THE

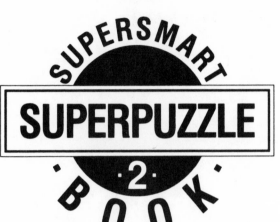

SUPERSMART

SUPERPUZZLE

·2·

BOOK

Also by Abbie F. Salny

Supersmart Superpuzzle Book

THE

SUPERSMART

SUPERPUZZLE

·2·

·BOOK·

ABBIE F. SALNY, ED.D.

A DELL BOOK

A DELL TRADE PAPERBACK

Published by
Dell Publishing
a division of
Bantam Doubleday Dell Publishing Group, Inc.
666 Fifth Avenue
New York, New York 10103

The trademark Dell ® is registered in the U.S. Patent and Trademark Office.

ISBN: 0-440-50409-0

Printed in the United States of America

To Jerry, for all the best reasons

INTRODUCTION

Here it is! The second collection of supersmart puzzles for your enjoyment and puzzlement is ready. You will find some old favorite types, but there are some new and unusual puzzles included also. Have a good time. Happy puzzling.

ABBIE SALNY

PUZZLES

1 It is possible to rearrange the same nine letters to fill in the blanks below. One is a nine-letter word, the other is a two-word combination.

Despite the proverb, it is the better part of _ _ _ _ _ _ _ _ _ to inspect a _ _ _ _ _ _ _ _ _ _.

2 Fill in each of the following definitions. Then take the first letter of each word you have filled in and rearrange the letters to fill in the boxes. When put in the right order they will form a word. The definitions are off-beat: puns or anagrams.

Ice cream or style _ _ _ _ _
Talk about a mechanical approach! _ _ _ _ _ _
Usually jugged _ _ _ _ _
A number with a cockney accent _ _ _ _ _ _ _
A cowardly "fellow" _ _ _ _ _ _ _
Unwind with a t _ _ _ _ _ _

WORD: ⬚⬚⬚⬚⬚⬚

3 At the local recycling plant they are very good about using up every bit of scrap. From every seven bottles they can make one new one. How many new bottles can they make after recycling 221 bottles?

4 Which of the following is the odd man out?

ETHEL   LAURA   THERESA   CORNELIA   GWENDOLYN

5 Compose a palindrome (example: Madam, I'm Adam) about Edna and Enid and what they did when they went out for the evening.

____ ___ ____ ____

6 There was a really big prize for guessing the number of peanuts piled up in the sack in the store window: two free tickets to the circus. Al guessed 110, Sam guessed 115, Bill guessed 108, and Jerry guessed 118. They were wrong, not in the order given, by two, by five, by three, and by five. How many peanuts were in the pile?

7 The following wheel with six spokes has five circles in it. Each spoke contains a jumbled word, with the same missing letter for each word in the middle circle. Find the missing letter and unscramble the words.

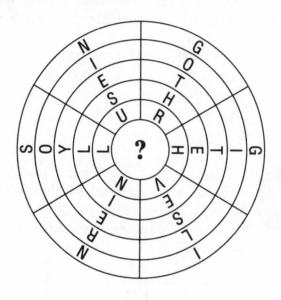

8 There is, as far as we can tell, only one other word that can be made by using all the letters in ENUMERATION. What is it?

9 Below is a sum using all the digits from 1 to 9, in which the answer is 927. There are three other ways, using only the digits 1 to 9 for the entire problem, to get the same result. Find the other three ways. (Each must be a completely new addition example. That is, you may not simply reverse the top and bottom sets of numbers.)

346	XXX	XXX	XXX
+581	+ XXX	+ XXX	+ XXX
927	927	927	927

10 Fill in the missing number below. Each design has been assigned a value. When you figure out the value you will be able to replace the question mark with the correct number.

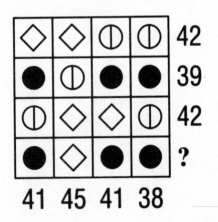

11 There is a most unusual clothing store where the proprietor prices goods according to a logic all his own. For example, he sells a dress for $65. He sells shoes for $66, and he sells a hat for $29. How much will he charge for a blouse?

12 Another palindrome. This one concerns Edna and her friend, who are engaging in a form of dance.

___ ___ ____ ___

13 Five men had a race at the annual picnic of the Associated Widget and Dingbat factory. They were, not in order, Tom, John, Bill, Pat, and Kevin. Pat was neither first nor last. Kevin was four behind the winner. Bill beat Pat, John came in after Tom, but ahead of Pat. Bill was neither first nor second. Tom was not second or third. Give the rankings.

14 The following coiled sentence contains a profound truth. Start at the correct letter, move to any touching letter, and you will find a mystery unfolding.

```
V E O E T
E U Y L P
R Y S L A
H T R O M
I N A A D
G E X R T
E C O E I
P O T F D
T H W O L
```

15 The same eight letters can be rearranged to fill in the blanks. Can you fill them in?

The play was a genuine tragedy, with spectacular stage effects. At the end, the illusion that you actually saw the heroine _ _ _ _ _ _ _ _ was perfect. There wasn't a dry eye in the house as it came time to _ _ _ _   _ _ _ _ the final curtain.

16 In the following poem you must select a letter from each line as indicated. When you have finished you will have a new word, reading the letters in order.

My first is in pansy, but not in rose,
My second in run, but not in goes.
My third is in daze, but not in muddle,
My fourth in haze, but not in puddle.
My fifth is in little, also in small,
My last in tumble, but not in fall.
My whole an amusement, so some guess,
To others, nothing but a mess.

17 The beautiful princess lived in the land inhabited by those perennial puzzle favorites, the Liars and the Truthtellers. The princess was herself a Truthteller and had no wish to marry a Liar. When a handsome young man from far away in the same land asked for her hand in marriage, she devised a simple test to find out whether or not he was a Liar. She said to him, as they were sitting in the garden one day, "Do you see that woman walking in the road? I've never seen her before, but I would like to have her as a maid—she looks very nice. Go and ask her if she is a Truthteller or a Liar." The young man returned and said, "She says she is a Truthteller," which solved the problem for the princess very nicely. Was the handsome (and rich) young man a Liar or a Truthteller, and how can you tell with certainty?

18 In another area of Puzzle Land fierce winds blow all the time, sometimes in one direction, sometimes in the other. A fast train— or reasonably fast, depending on your ideas—can run under its own steam, if forced, 100 mph between Never-Never and Sometimes. This particular day it picked up a very strong favorable breeze that doubled its speed to 200 mph, at which speed the train completed its two-hundred-mile journey in one hour. At the usual time the train had to make the return journey. Unfortunately, the same wind was still blowing in the same direction at the same speed. How fast would the engineer have to push the train to make the journey home in four hours?

19 My clocks have gone crazy since the electrical failure apparently damaged them. The one in the kitchen is three minutes per hour slow, and the one in the living room is three minutes per hour fast. In how many hours from the time they started will they be exactly one hour apart? (And why didn't I take them to be repaired?)

20 In the supermarket you meet your mother's only brother-in-law's only brother-in-law. What do you call the gentleman?

21 What is the five-digit number, no zeros, in which the first number is one-fourth the second, the second is twice the third, the third is two-thirds of the fourth, and the fifth is half of the fourth, with the sum of all the digits being twenty-three?

22 The names of two countries are hidden in the following two sentences. The letters of each country are sequential and in the proper order. Find the countries.

Both Interpol and the FBI had found a clue. There was a hidden mark on the map the suspect was carrying, which might mark a rendezvous.

23 The same ten letters can be rearranged as shown to fill in the sentences below.

In the past, a man who had _ _ _ _ _ _ _ _ _ _ could not be executed again if the execution failed. Sometimes the gallows _ _ _ _ _ _ _ _ _ _ and he was set free.

24 There is an eight-letter word that has been arranged in the box below. You must determine whether it can be read clockwise or counterclockwise and which is the starting letter.

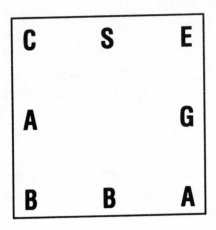

C S E

A G

B B A

25 The following five letters can be used to make at least six English words, using all letters. Some may be slightly unusual, but they are in the dictionary. How many can you find?

A I L R S

26 The name of a bird is hidden in each of the following sentences. All of the letters are in the correct order and in sequence. Find the birds.

I order you to stop fighting over that roast turkey, and I want you to put back that leg, Reta.
That man has been much maligned; he's not an ogre, be certain of that.
Eric, rake that lawn before I come out and make you do it!

27 Each of the following groups of letters has one thing in common, with one exception. Unscramble the words and find the exception.

FLAC   TLPOU   TSHAO   EVERTLE   RTUYKE

28 At the employment agency a very nice-looking young man appeared for his interview and seemed quite troubled. The interviewer asked him why, and he explained that he had been sitting next to another candidate, who had bragged that he was a Liar and would deceive the interviewer. The interviewer, well used to life in the land of the Liars and the Truthtellers, smiled to himself and did not hire the young man. Why?

29 It really isn't very late, I thought to myself. As a matter of fact, if it were only one hour later, it would be twice as long to midnight as it would be if it were two hours later. What time was it when I thought this?

30 The following coiled phrase can be uncoiled by starting at the correct letter and moving in any direction to a touching letter. It will finish the rhyme, A MAN WHO SMILES WHEN THINGS GO WRONG:

```
W O F O J
R O B S I
V E N H E
R Y L T V
G N O A H
```

31 Grandfather has very strong likes and dislikes. He likes his neighbor Mr. Newsome, but not his neighbor Mr. Smith. He likes grapefruit but not apples. He likes baseball but not soccer. In accordance with his likes and dislikes, will he visit Ireland or France?

32 No experienced skater is graceless.
Katie is always tripping and falling down.
No graceful person is always tripping and falling down.

What can you tell about Katie?

33 The name of a fruit is hidden in each of the sentences below. Find the fruit.

"You are truly a detestable person," said the fellow to his neighbor, "and you are a cur, ranting and raving about my little child!"

It was too bad that we had so much trouble at Thanksgiving, but all the relatives pitched in to help with the pump; kin are supposed to help out.

Take off your cap, please, you are in a religious center.

34 An oft-misquoted saying is coiled at the end of this rhyming sentence. There are three null letters. IN ERROR OFTEN, PEOPLE QUOTE THIS THING:

```
L T T D A
E L I A N
E A L S G
R N A I E
I N G R O
x G I S U
x x N H T
```

35
It is possible to replace the first letter of each pair of words shown below with a different letter, turning the words into two new words. The letter used should be placed on the line between the two new words. If you choose correctly you will have a new word composed of the letters on the middle line, reading down.

CHIP _____ BANE
NOTION _____ CORE
SIDE _____ LISLE
DEAD _____ COWED
GOWN _____ CRASH

36
A certain logic has been followed in the sequence below. Pick the group below the sequence that best continues the series:

a)  b) c)

37 The following word square consists of four words that can be read the same across or down. One word has been filled in for you.
Complete the square by using, in addition to the words shown, the letters O, O, O, O, R, R, D, L, T.

C O S T
O
S
T

38 There is an eight-letter word contained in the segments below. One letter has been omitted. Fill in the missing letter and read the word. (The word may have been inserted either clockwise or counterclockwise.)

39 The Great Detective had caught up with the criminal after many years. (In those days nobody minded how long things took.) "No," said the alleged criminal, "I was at a house party that Saturday, away in the country. I spent February 29, 1900, at the home of the duchess. Here's my diary and a list of the guests." The Great Detective arrested him immediately. Why?

40 Another couple of palindromes, like Madam, I'm Adam.

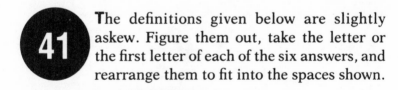

What the Dutchman did with his extra milk supply:

———— ————

First appearance of a would-be star on television:

———— —————

41 The definitions given below are slightly askew. Figure them out, take the letter or the first letter of each of the six answers, and rearrange them to fit into the spaces shown.

Tear King Canute's nemesis.
She said, "I have a fishy tale."
It's a long way from DOWN to here.
A close associate of C's.
If we didn't have this one, it would be hard to have more than one.
Most frequent letter.

WORD: □□□□□□□

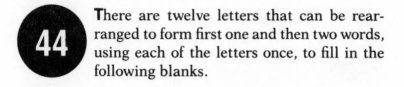

42 Each of the following words has at least three of the same vowels removed. There is a different vowel for every word.

EXTRVGNZ   TLGRAPHR   PRPRTINAL

43 Give the five-digit number, no zeros, in which the first digit is the sum of the last two digits, the second digit is twice the first digit and three times the fourth digit, and the total for all five digits is sixteen.

44 There are twelve letters that can be rearranged to form first one and then two words, using each of the letters once, to fill in the following blanks.

After the accident the research team decided the area was

——————————.

All future visitors were greeting with a warning:

—— ——————————.

45 Without resorting to any sort of magic, can you change beer to wine in only eight steps? You must change one letter at a time, making a proper English word with each change.

```
B     E     E     R

___   ___   ___   ___

___   ___   ___   ___

___   ___   ___   ___

___   ___   ___   ___

___   ___   ___   ___

___   ___   ___   ___

W     I     N     E
```

46 A different letter has been taken out of each of the eight-letter words below. Note, of course, that now there are seven letters or less in each word. Find the missing letter and unscramble each word. All are related to one subject, to give you a clue.

CDRLA   HNNSV   LDAEEAR   IIIOSN

47 The Ladies Handicrafts Circle met once a week. Unfortunately, some of them could only meet on Monday and others only on Wednesday. Four of the Monday group and three of the Wednesday group managed to make as many potholders in five days as three of the Monday group and five of the Wednesday group made in four days. Which group, Monday or Wednesday, contained faster workers?

48 Four years ago Jane was twice as old as Alice. In four more years Alice will be two-thirds of Jane's age now. How old is Alice now?

49 What number should replace the question mark?

50 You can make a six-letter word (one letter may be used more than once) by NOT using any of the letters shown.

B C D E
F G H I
J M P Q
R S T U
V W Y Z

― ― ― ― ― ―

51 A series of words is given below. Can you select the word that fits the pattern and continues the series from the lettered words? (Hint: It has nothing to do with meanings, number of letters, or syllables.)

PEACH ENDLESS DARLING LIGHTNING TRIUMPH
a) wisdom b) pine c) history d) rhythm

52 As far as we can tell, there is only one anagram for the word POSITIONAL. What is it?

53 Some of these puzzles seem to be quite old. This one is adapted from a type that must have been around for hundreds of years. You have two types of candles, which burn at different rates of speed. If you light them both at the same time, in one hour one is three-fifths of its original length, and the other is four-fifths of its original length. In how many more hours will the original faster-burning candle go out?

54 Find the next number(s) in the following sequence:

98   89   73   52

55 What comes next in the series to replace the question marks?

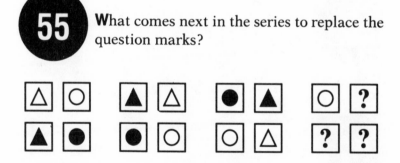

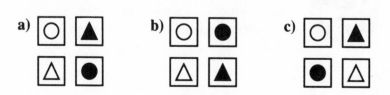

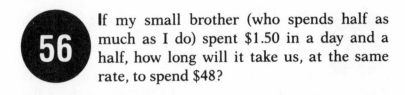 If my small brother (who spends half as much as I do) spent $1.50 in a day and a half, how long will it take us, at the same rate, to spend $48?

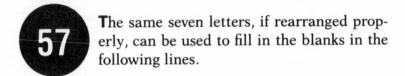 The same seven letters, if rearranged properly, can be used to fill in the blanks in the following lines.

The fact that the waitress in the Wild West Saloon spilled
___ ____ down the back of his lady's dress led to a full-scale row by the prospector. This eventually led to a _____-__ and several arrests.

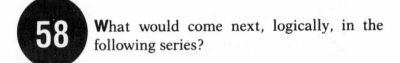 What would come next, logically, in the following series?

J. 31, F. 28, M. 31

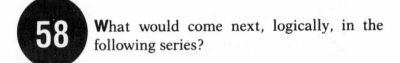 What two numbers will give you an answer of 36 when one is subtracted from the other and 1,440 when they are multiplied?

60 The car thieves had a rough time of it. They had to go a slow, crawling, fourteen miles per hour because the logging road was very bad. They finally stopped, after twenty-eight miles, to wait until daylight. Unfortunately, they didn't realize that they had punctured the gas tank and left a trail of gasoline behind them. They had run over a sharp stone right at the dying campfire, where they had stolen the vehicle while the campers slept. The trail of gas had caught fire and was burning steadily at a nice twelve miles per hour. How long were the miscreants—or "perps"—going to have to wait for their stunning surprise?

61 There is a very common English word that can be made from the letters on the top row of a standard typewriter. For those of you who do not have a typewriter keyboard handy for reference, the letters are Q, W, E, R, T, Y, U, I, O, P. Not all letters must be used and some letters may be used more than once.

62 A coward could redeem himself by going from FEAR to BOLD. You can do this in five steps, changing one letter at each step to make a new, proper English word:

F   E   A   R

___ ___ ___ ___

___ ___ ___ ___

___ ___ ___ ___

B   O   L   D

63 Here is the signpost one unlucky traveler found. He was walking and he was very tired. Unfortunately, the signpost to DEVON, where he wanted to go, was illegible. How far was it to DEVON?

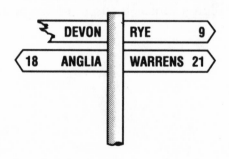

64 The following famous quote has had all the vowels taken out and the remaining letters broken up into groups of four. There are two null letters. Put the quote together again.

NTHS PRNG YNGM NSFN CYLG HTLY TRNS
TTHG HTSF LVxx

65 Another cryptic poem.

My first is in toy, but not in play,
My second in sun, but not in day.
My third is in light, but not in dark,
My fourth in listen, but not in hark.
My last in picture, not in frame,
My whole is just a flower's name.

66 Each of the following words can be made into another word by having the *same* four-letter word placed in front of it. Find the four-letter word and make the new words.

_ _ _ _ MARK
_ _ _ _ WORM
_ _ _ _ MAN

27

67 How many common, six-letter words can you make from the letters A, C, E, N, S, T? Each letter may be used only once and all the letters must be used. You should be able to find four—there may be more, but these are the most common.

68 Old Mother Hubbard's cupboard was, as we all know, bare—no news to anyone. She did have a little money left and went off to buy some bread and milk. She bought a loaf of bread and a quart of milk for $2.50, paying $1 less for the milk than for the bread. How much did the milk cost?

69 What comes next in the following series?

ONE   ELEVEN   NINE   EIGHT   THIRTY-SEVEN
a) sixteen   b) forty-eight   c) ninety   d) thirty-three

70 There is a family gathering and someone (probably an in-law) tries to introduce you to your only brother's wife's only sister-in-law's husband. What do you say?

71 What is the five-digit number in which the first digit is two-thirds of the second, the third is one-third of the second, the fourth is four times the last, and the last is one-third the first. The digits total twenty-eight.

72 A very large dog was placed on a household scale. The owner saw that the very large dog weighed seventy-five pounds plus half its weight, or at least that's what he told his wife, who thought he fed the dog too much. How much did the dog really weigh?

73 The carpenter was in a terrible hurry. He had to work as fast as possible, but he had to cut a heavy ten-foot plank into ten equal sections. He knew it took him one minute per cut. How long would it take him to finish the job?

74 Each of the drawings below is of the same cube. A different letter has been placed on each of the six faces. Figure out which letter is on the bottom of each of the six drawings, and then rearrange the letters to form a word.

75

Very few of us now have dial telephones, but the letter and number system is the same as it was when telephone dials were used for codes. Here is a code message based on a telephone numbering system. For example, 2 would equal *A*, *B*, or *C*. All you have to do is select the correct letter from each group of three to solve the puzzle.

8447   47   4273   2322873   84373   273   84733
2464237   367   3224   686237

76

The following Terse Verse will rhyme when you figure out the coiled sentence. There is one null letter.
OLD MOTHER HUBBARD WENT TO THE CUPBOARD TO GET HER POOR DOG A BONE.

```
B U H A N D A M E
T T E R G E R A L
O O D L T D E Y B
R B E L H R O P H
L C T A D H D N O
E V E R O G A E x
```

77 At the college reunion a group of men and women were discussing their lives after they had received their undergraduate degrees. It turned out that everybody in the group had gone on to receive an advanced degree, so each of them had two degrees. Each degree holder had both a B.A. and an M.S., an M.A., an M.B.A., or an M.F.A. Half of them had an M.S., one-quarter had an M.A., one-sixth had an M.B.A., and just one had an M.F.A. How many were there in total?

78 Some things are enough to scare anyone. You might be able to go from WARM to COLD quite easily, but how about from COLD to WARM? Can you change one letter at a time and make a proper English word with each step? You should be able to do it in four steps.

C   O   L   D

___   ___   ___   ___

___   ___   ___   ___

W   A   R   M

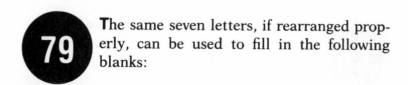

79 The same seven letters, if rearranged properly, can be used to fill in the following blanks:

Mrs. Gotrocks was complaining about her new cook, very bitterly. "My cook _ _ _ _ _ _ _ eggs the wrong way," she said. "I've told her and told her and _ _ _ _ _ _ _, but I still don't get my breakfast eggs the way I want them."

80 A palindrome (example: Madam, I'm Adam) can be tricky. This one is about the maternal parent giving her daughter Edna a specific piece, or cut, of meat.

_ _   _ _ _ _ _ _   _ _ _ _   _ _ _

81 Now that you are in the palindromic mode, perhaps you could try another. Lisa was extremely upset about Delia's illness.

_ _ _ _ _   _ _ _   _ _ _,   _ _ _ _   _ _ _ _ _ _

82 The same nine letters, rearranged, can be used to fill in the blanks below to make a reasonably sensible sentence.

The man from Outer Space was staying with a resident of Earth as part of a hospitality visit. It was his first morning, and he was watching his host with considerable interest. "Tell me, _ _ _ _ _ _ _ _ _," he said, patting his hairless visage, "why are you _ _ _ _ _ _ _ _ _ your face?"

83 There is one four-letter word that can be placed before each of the following words to make a new word. Fill in the correct four-letter word.

_ _ _ _ REAL
_ _ _ _ WAYS
_ _ _ _ SLIP
_ _ _ _ SWIPE

84 An interesting statement below has had all the vowels removed and has been broken up into groups of three letters that are not the actual words. There is one null letter. Reconstitute the saying.

CMM   TTS   GRP   WHC   HKP   SMN   TSB   TWS
TSH   RSx

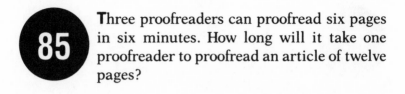

85 Three proofreaders can proofread six pages in six minutes. How long will it take one proofreader to proofread an article of twelve pages?

86 This one's an oldie, but perhaps you haven't run into it yet. What English word can have four of its five letters removed and still retain the same pronunciation?

87 The following multiplication problem uses each digit from 0 to 9 once and only once in the problem and in the answer (not in the intermediate steps). Only one number has been filled in. Complete the arithmetic example. (No multiplication sign has been included.)

```
      X X X
        7 X
  _____
    X X X X X
```

88 When Jim came home from school to the diner his father owned, he found it in disorder. His father was not there, so Jim went into the kitchen and found the chef had left. He called his father and said:

```
  P O P
  P O P
    N O
-------
C O O K
```

You can replace each of the letters with a number and come up with a correct addition example. (Hint: P = 7.)

89 You are in the land of the Liars and Truthtellers again, and you need a Truthteller desperately for a business deal you are working on. You go to a business lunch with three men, each of whom is in the same business, and you ask if any of them is a Truthteller. The first one says, "There are three Truthtellers here." The second says, "No, only one of us is a Truthteller," and the third one answers, "The second man is telling the truth." Well, what are they: Liars, Truthtellers, or a mixture, and how many of each?

90 Spring cleaning day has arrived, and as a reward for your hard work you have found $3.60 under the sofa cushions. It's in quarters, dimes, and pennies, equal numbers of each. How many of each are there?

91 The following sad statement was penned by a job applicant who had taken a series of tests but was not hired. He complained to his friend, "They consider the job a multiple choice test . . ." (Unscramble the square to complete the sentence.)

```
T O E N
H F O M
E A N A
B V N I
O E D A
```

92 Given the current state of the economy the Johnson family decides to visit Grandma and Grandpa for their vacation, instead of spending money at a hotel. (We are not told how Grandma and Grandpa feel about eight visitors in their California condo.) They are in no hurry, so the first day they drive one-half the total distance. The next day there are a lot of sight-seeing attractions en route and they drive one-third of the remaining miles. On the third day there are a few national parks, and they cover one-third of the remaining distance. Upon looking at the map they find they have sixty-four miles to go. How far have they driven so far?

93 One must work to live, obviously (but it's not obvious to everybody, so don't point it out). Can you change TOIL into FOOD in only three steps, changing one letter at a time to make a new English word each time? (example: CAP, CAT, HAT)

T   O   I   L

___ ___ ___ ___

___ ___ ___ ___

F   O   O   D

94 By picking the correct letter from each clue given, you can spell out a five-letter word.

My first is in day, but not in night,
My second in flame, but not in light.
My third is in milk, but not in tea,
My fourth in slip, but not in plea.
My last in yellow, not in whale,
My whole for love will tell a tale.

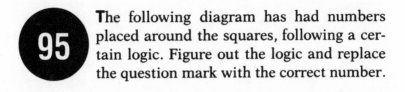

95 The following diagram has had numbers placed around the squares, following a certain logic. Figure out the logic and replace the question mark with the correct number.

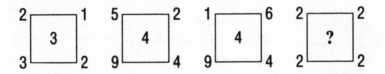

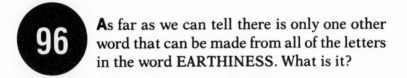

96 As far as we can tell there is only one other word that can be made from all of the letters in the word EARTHINESS. What is it?

97 "Shop till you drop" took on a new meaning when Ellen and Sue went shopping. In the first store they went into they were tempted and spent half the money they had brought. In the second store they spent four-fifths of what they had left. In the third store they spent four-fifths of what was left. At that point they had a load of shopping bags and five dollars left, just enough to pay for coffee and cake before starting home. How much had they started out with?

98 The following brief palindrome (a word or phrase that reads the same backward as forward) should be a relief to those worried about Australian wildlife.

— — — — —   — —

99 Unfortunately, your husband seems to be color-blind. You've seen him wearing one brown sock and one blue sock for two days now. He says he has another pair just like it in the sock drawer. Deciding to simplify his life, you manage to get him to agree to wear only brown socks, blue socks, and black socks. His sock drawer now contains these colors in a ratio of four black socks to three brown socks to five blue socks. How many socks does he have to take out of the drawer now in order to be sure that he has a pair of the correct matching color?

100 Fill in the missing number outside the square below.

A	C	D	B	10
A	C	A	B	7
D	B	A	B	9
D	A	C	B	10

9 10 9 9 8 ?

101 What is the five-digit number in which the last number is the product of the first and second, the last number is twice the second, the fourth is the sum of the third and the last, and the sum of all the digits is twenty-four?

40

102 A certain system has been used to place the letters around the squares below. Figure out the system and fill in the missing letter.

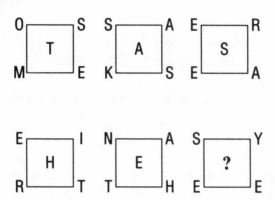

O   S   S   A   E   R
   T   A   S
M   E   K   S   E   A

E   I   N   A   S   Y
   H   E   ?
R   T   T   H   E   E

103 A palindrome reads the same backward as forward. (Madam, I'm Adam.) Here's a rather complicated palindrome involving Sharon, Marge, and Norah, wherein Marge allows one of the others to see a message not addressed to her.

_ _ _ _ _   _ _ _ _   _ _ _ _ _   _ _ _   _ _ _ _ _ _ _ ' _

_ _ _ _ _ _ _ _

104 The names of three birds are hidden in the sentences below. The letters are in their proper order and are consecutive in forming the names.

That animal won't bite. All the others do, but not that one.
Hush, Rik, even the neighbors are complaining about your screaming.
Ring, mailman, ring! Rouse the sleeper from his slumber!

105 Two of the pieces below *cannot* be used to make a circle. All of the remaining pieces, if put together, will form a circle. Which two don't fit?

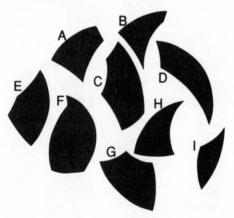

106 What is the English language word most often pronounced wrong?

107 Change the first letter of each word below—the same letter for each pair with a line between them. Insert the new letter on the line. When you have done all the words correctly, you will have a new word, reading down.

GOWN _____ SAIL
COME _____ WALE
ROTA _____ UNTO
RODE _____ RICE
RING _____ MISS

108 The following line consists of the names of three famous authors interlettered. All the letters of each name are in the correct order, but other letters are between them. Find the three authors.

S K K I W P E I L N A I B T N U S R G N E

109 Why are 1991 silver dollars worth more than 1990 silver dollars?

110 Can you change MEAT to BONE by changing one letter at a time to form a new English word? The fewest steps we've been able to manage is five. Can you match or better this?

M	E	A	T
___	___	___	___
___	___	___	___
___	___	___	___
B	O	N	E

111 The following Terse Verse ends with a coiled sentence. When you uncoil the sentence by moving from letter to letter in any direction where successive letters touch (including corners), you will find the rest of the verse.

SUCCESS IS A MATTER OF LUCK, YOU KNOW.

```
A T U I L U
S S J A E R
K A F H E W
S U L L T I
O O Y E L L
```

112 Each of the following scrambled words is a girl's name—except one. Which one is the odd woman out?

MTLLIINCE   AULRA   AAEINNGL   UAKRQ

113 It was a very minor sort of lottery. Roger, the owner of the local candy store, had a guessing contest to see who could tell how many jelly beans were in the container in the window. Sue guessed 92, William guessed 88, Jane guessed 95, Alice guessed 87, and Jack guessed 101. They were wrong, not in the order given, by six, eight, three, and seven, and one of them was correct. How many jelly beans were there?

114 A palindrome reads the same backward as forward (Madam, I'm Adam). In this palindrome Otto is preparing a nice, soothing rubdown for Lew.

— — — ,   — — — —   — — —   —   — — —   — — — — —

115 Christmas shopping season was open. Mrs. Gotbucks was out in the stores. In the first she spent half of everything she had with her, plus two dollars. In the second she spent half of what was left, plus one dollar. In the third she spent half of everything she had left, and then had seven dollars. What had she started with?

45

116 It's not polite to ask a lady's age, but that never stops visitors from asking little girls. This particular little girl said, "Five years ago my younger sister was exactly three-fifths of my age. Six years from now she'll be seven-eighths of my age. When we're both grown-up, in twenty years, say, she'll only be fourteen-fifteenths of my age." How old were the little girl and her sister at the time the visitor asked the question?

117 Still another palindrome (Madam, I'm Adam): Tessa is voyaging abroad, where her facility in a classical language is of some help.

_ _ _ _ _ ' _   _ _   _ _ _ _ _ ,   _ _ _ _ _   _ _

_ _ _ _ _

118 Each of the following words can be rescrambled (not like an egg, but in recognizable form) to create a new word, relating to food, that uses all of the same letters.

CONTOURS   BRUTE   SPEAR   CHECK-IN   ENVIED

119 We're back in the land of the Liars and Truthtellers again. This time you meet two men dressed differently (by which you are able to tell one is a Liar and the other a Truthteller). The first man says, "I am a Truthteller, he is a Liar." The second man says, "Yes, he is telling the truth about being a Truthteller, but I am not a Liar." Which is which and why?

120 The following puzzle is really quite simple. Complete the missing line:

SAM   = 1 2 3
ARTIE = 2 4 5 6 7
SMART = ?

121 The recycling process was in full swing in one small town. From every twenty-four cans that were turned in they were able to get one new can. To date, this week 1,728 cans have been turned in. How many new cans will they wind up with at the end of the entire cycle, just from those 1,728?

122 There is a country hidden in each of the sentences or group of sentences below, one country to each set. The letters are in consecutive order.

"That gorilla must weigh a ton." "Gabons usually weigh a ton, not gorillas," he said.
Beer is made of malt. Another ingredient is hops.
He's gone, pal, there's no use looking for him.

123 What relationship to you is your father's mother-in-law's only daughter's only child?

124 Supply the missing numbers to fill in the sequence.

_ _ 9 27 _ 243

125 Each of the symbols in the boxes below has been assigned a number. Figure out what each number is and complete the row with the question mark.

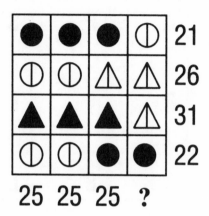

25 25 25 ?

126 Sally's sister Susie has some very odd likes and dislikes. She will ride in a cab, but not a taxi. She will talk to no one, but not to you. She will eat pasta, but not rice. She will turn left or right, but not around. Will she like tulips or roses?

49

127 An eight-letter word has been arranged in a square below. All you have to do is decipher the word. Start at any letter and move clockwise or counterclockwise.

128 Edward Lear seems to have invented this type of "word ladder," in which one letter at a time is changed in order to turn one word into another (example: CAP, CAT, MAT). Can you change WORD into DEED in only four steps?

```
W   O   R   D
___ ___ ___ ___
___ ___ ___ ___
___ ___ ___ ___
D   E   E   D
```

129 Each of the following words has at least three of the same vowel missing. (The vowel varies from word to word.) Reconstruct the words.

PRSSS BRCDBR PHMRA PRSNTABL NVGLATED

130 Now for a brief spot of creativity. Each of the following words is part of several other words or word combinations. For example, BACK might be used for BACKHAND, BACKWARD, LINEBACK, and so on. Try to give four combinations for each of the words shown.

SOFT   POST   DOOR   READ

131 Study the part indicated for Figure 1 and decide which part matches Figure 2.

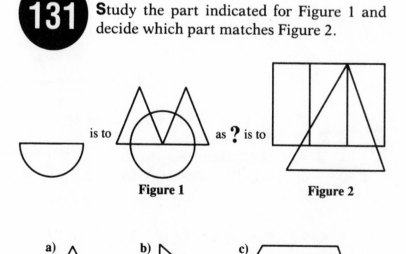

is to ... as **?** is to

Figure 1   Figure 2

a)   b)   c)

51

132 There is quite a difference in age between the oldest and youngest sisters in the family. If you add their ages together you get ninety-one, but of course that's not much help. However, it is possible to tell you that the older sister is now twice as old as the younger sister was when the older sister was the age that the younger sister is now. The difference in their ages is one-fourth the age of the older sister. How old are the sisters?

133 Still another word change. Can you change one letter at a time, making a proper English word at each step, and go from LONG to WIDE in only five steps?

L	O	N	G
―	―	―	―
―	―	―	―
W	I	D	E

134 The following cryptogram is a spoof. It is a well-known saying with a twist and is quite easy. It is taken from the (imaginary) book of "Household Rules by One Who Knows Better."

24 15 22 26 13 15 18 13 22 8 8   18 8   13 22 3 7
7 12   18 14 11 12 8 8 18 25 15 22

135 By using all the digits from 0 to 9 it is possible to construct one multiplication example (the single use of the digits is only for the problem and the answer, not the intermediate steps). Here is such a problem. Fill in the numbers. One number has been filled in to get you started.

$$
\begin{array}{r}
\_\ \_\ \_ \\
\times \quad \_\ \_ \\
\hline
\_\ \_\ \_\ \_\ \ 1 \\
\end{array}
$$

136 The following Terse Verse can be read and completed in the coiled square below. There are two null letters.

THE MATH TEACHER SAID, "THERE'S A RULE QUITE STRONG:"

```
I I S O N E x
T F E U O I x
C O M T D T G
H G I R E W N
T Y O U V R O
```

137 Samantha and Sally went off on a shopping spree. They started out with a certain number of dollars. They spent fifty percent of their money in the first store, twenty-five percent of the original amount in the second store,

fourteen percent in the third, and five percent of the
original amount in the last store. At that point they had
six dollars left and were exhausted, so they spent it on
a bargain movie matinee. How much had they started
out with?

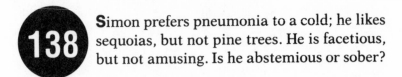

Simon prefers pneumonia to a cold; he likes
sequoias, but not pine trees. He is facetious,
but not amusing. Is he abstemious or sober?

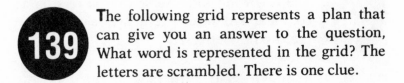

The following grid represents a plan that
can give you an answer to the question,
What word is represented in the grid? The
letters are scrambled. There is one clue.

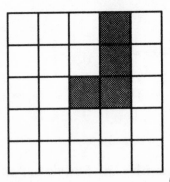

Z

140 Royal Relatives: Cross out the letters as indicated, and you'll find your answer.

If Henry VIII of England called Ferdinand and Isabella mother-in-law and father-in-law, cross out all the *S*'s. If not, cross out all the *R*'s and *I*'s.

If Queen Elizabeth I called Mary, Queen of Scots, cousin, cross out all the *M*'s, *E*'s, and *A*'s. If not, cross out the *H*'s.

If Kaiser Wilhelm and King George V were cousins, cross out all the *L*'s, *Z*'s, *O*'s, and *U*'s. If not, cross out all the *T*'s.

If Prince Philip was Greek, cross out all the *W*'s. If not, cross out all the *G*'s.

Z R S M W I S M L G Z S M W H Z A E T E U O O L M

141 If you change the last letter of each of the pairs of words shown below and place it in the brackets between the pairs of words, you will have a new word reading down. (Example: DIN could be changed to DIG.)

```
WENT  _____  RAIL
PERT  _____  SKY
ARID  _____  DIVE
HALE  _____  GOAD
```

142 Each of the following lines of words can have one word placed in front of each word to make a new word. The number of letters is shown for the new word for each line.

3 letters: ROCK, ROLL, POST
3 letters: STONE, PUNCH, HOLE
5 letters: HAIR, BACK, PLAY

143 The following is a famous proverb cloaked in excess verbiage. Try to figure out the original expression.

A small coin, of equally small value, when secluded or stored in such a manner as to accrue interest to the owner at a later date actually represents the same amount of money acquired by gainful employment or other source of income.

144 Just to make things more fun at the small party, there was a small raffle prize. Groups chipped in, and one group won. If there had been two more people in the group, each would have received one dollar less and there would have been two dollars left over. If there had been twice as many in that group, each would have won $2.50 less. If there had been three less, each one would have received two dollars more and there would have been one dollar left. How many were there in the winning group, and what did each one win? Each one got even dollars, with nothing left over.

145 The same ten letters can be rearranged into two words to fit each of the blanks shown. Read the sentence, decide on the ten letters, make each group of ten letters into two words, and fill in the blanks to make sense.

"I was on a very _ _ _ _ _ _   _ _ _ _," said the tearful young woman.
"It consisted of white wine and fruit only, and it worked wonderfully well, until just now, when I realize I must have been exceeding the _ _ _ _ _   _ _ _ _ _."

146 When I rechecked my monthly charge bill I found an interesting mathematical relationship among the four things I had bought. The first cost one-third as much as the third, which cost double the second, which in turn cost as much as the fourth. The total was twenty-eight dollars. How much was each item?

147 You have a very, very important appointment in Never-Never Land. You have to pick up your aged mother at exactly 2:00 P.M. She lives in a village that has a dragon guarding the gates except for a brief period before and after 2:00 P.M., when you can safely pick her up. If you leave at 10:00 A.M. you'll be too early by an hour, and it's dangerous to hang around. If you leave at noon you'll be an hour too late, and your poor mother will be gone. What's the speed of your magicmobile, which can only travel at that specific speed?

148 There is a pattern in the following sequence. Fill in the missing number.

38 22 8 16 14 10 2 4 8 16 14 _ 2

149 The poor dress designer. He had relied on brand-new packers to ship to the store that had ordered dresses and they had done a bad job. The store called up and said, "Half of them are damaged, and twenty-six others are the wrong size. Only ninety-nine of the whole shipment are what we ordered." How many had they ordered?

150 There are three sets of definitions given below. Fill the line between with a word that means the same as both definitions (a different word for each line).

irritated or peeved _____ intersect
tumble   _____ time of year
benevolent   _____ type or sort

151 A magic square is a number square in which all the lines—across, down, and diagonal—add up to the same number. Here's a hard one, in which all the numbers add up to 15. Two numbers have been added to get you started. No number may be used twice.

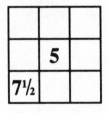

152 The "girls" from the office went out to lunch with their spouses, including two husbands and one wife, and, fortunately for some of them, agreed to separate checks. Couple A spent one-third of the total. Couple B felt expansive and had shrimp cocktail and filet mignon, and their bill was twice that of Couple A's, less ten dollars. On the other hand, Couple C was trying to economize and had only a sandwich and a cup of coffee each. Their bill was only one-fourth that of couple A's. How much was the total?

153 In this particular corner of Puzzle Land, two tortoises decided to race. Tortoise 1 raced at six miles per day, all day, regardless of the territory. Tortoise 2 raced at four miles per day uphill and eight miles per day downhill. The course was six miles up and six miles down, for a total of twelve miles. Which one won, and by how much?

154 As far as we can tell there is only one word that can be made by anagramming POLY-ESTER. What is it?

155 What number is one-half of two-thirds of twenty percent of 255?

156 The new and not very mathematically in-clined antique dealer was examining her unsold merchandise as the show drew to a close. "Well," she said to herself, "I'll sell this twenty-dollar vase for 25 percent off, because I sold the last one for twenty dollars and made 25 percent. That way I'll break even." How good—or bad—was her math?

In the following math puzzle you can replace each letter with a number, and the example will be correct.

$$\begin{array}{r} A\ B\ C\ D\ E\ F\ G\ I \\ \times\quad\quad\quad\ I \\ \hline A\ A\ A\ A\ A\ A\ A\ A \end{array}$$

The names of three trees are hidden in the following sentences. The words are in correct sequence in each case.

If you have a sore toe it helps to soak it in hot water, which requires no cash outlay.
While playing in the cellar, children found a figure of an ancient man.
Don't race, darling, you will owe the doctor another bill if you fall.

159

It's easy to go from WORK to PLAY, but can you go from PLAY to WORK with as little trouble? Change one letter at a time, making a proper English word at each step. Try eight steps.

```
P   L   A   Y
___ ___ ___ ___
___ ___ ___ ___
___ ___ ___ ___
___ ___ ___ ___
___ ___ ___ ___
___ ___ ___ ___
___ ___ ___ ___
W   O   R   K
```

1

160

Three foods are interlettered in each of the following lines. Unscramble the edibles and find out what there is to eat.

APBAPENAAPNALCHE
BPVOEERAEKLF
SRQUBUTEAAESBTHAGA

161 The following two proverbs have had all the vowels removed and been broken into groups of four. Restore the proverbs to their original condition by inserting the proper vowels. There are two null letters.

```
B R D S   F F T H   R F L C   K T G T   H R x x
F L N D   H S M N   Y R S N   P R T D
```

162 Each of the following squares has been lettered according to a form of logic (I think!). Replace the question mark with the proper letter.

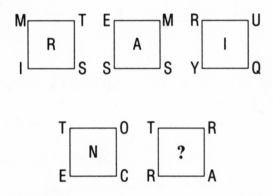

163 Fill in each of the following definitions. Then take the first letter of each word, place it in the correct position in the boxes, and you will have created a new word. For example, if the word definition was "Feline," you would write CAT in the blanks. *C* would then be one of the letters in the new word.

A girlish tempest _ _ _ _
In England, this game is called Snakes and _ _ _ _ _ _ _ _
Once brave, now a sandwich _ _ _ _ _
Amigo, I live here _ _ _ _
MacGregor of that _ _ _
If yesterday was Saturday, this will be Monday
_ _ _ _ _ _ _ _

WORD: ☐☐☐☐☐☐☐

164 The following multiplication example has one number given to get you started. All the digits from 0 to 9 are used in this puzzle (not including the intermediate steps). Fill in the missing digits. No multiplication sign has been used.

```
        7 X X
          X X
    _____
    X X X X X
```

165 The Great Detective was investigating a murder. The millionaire had died mysteriously, and his nephew, the chief suspect, had now come up with a will dated only a week earlier, which left everything to him. The Great Detective asked, "And just where did you find this new will?" The nephew replied, "I was sitting in the library, mourning my uncle, when I noticed on his desk a book opened facedown. I picked it up and there, between pages three and four, was this new will. He must have just written the will, had it witnessed by two strangers so that nobody would know, and been murdered shortly thereafter."

"Arrest that man immediately," said the Great Detective. How did he know the story wasn't true?

166 Which of the following words is the odd man out? It is not because they are birds or animals.

SHARK   EGRET   BREAM   SPIDER   PUPPY

167 The traffic was terrible on the way to Grandmother's house for Thanksgiving. The family averaged only 20 mph going out. On the way back it was a little better, and they averaged 30 mph. If the total time spent in the car going and coming back was five hours, how far away did Grandmother live?

168 If six widgets and three wonkles cost $21, and three widgets and six wonkles cost $24, how much does each widget and wonkle cost separately?

169 If three puzzle solvers can solve eighteen puzzles in a half hour, how many puzzle solvers will it take to solve seventy-two puzzles in one hour? (Please don't write in and tell me that not all puzzle solvers are equal. This is purely an assumption that holds true only in Puzzle Land.)

170 The same fifteen letters can be rearranged to form a new set of words, after you have found the first set. Fill in the blanks with the two sets of words.

While the referee was still _ _ _ _ _ _ _ _
_ _ _ _ _ _ _, the enraged player toppled his opponent
_ _ _ _ _ _ _ _ _ _ _ _ _ _ _.

171 What should come next in the following series? Pick the lettered group that best fits the sequence.

A Z B Y C X D W _ _ F U G T
a) M N   b) E W   c) E V   d) V E

172 The following saying has been put into multisyllabic words. Translate it back into the original English.

Individuals who are completely devoid of sapience in all respects indicate a propensity to cast themselves without hesitation onto those areas where beings of a heavenly nature would reflect seriously and be timorous about proceeding.

173 Which is the odd man out in this list of words?

ADOBE SALVE TOADY VIAND ALLOY TENET

174 Each of the following words has had at least three of the same letters removed. Replace the letters (a different one for each word) and find the originals.

COFROTIG   INAURAY   PRVNTABL

175 What is the five-digit number, no zeros, in which the last digit is five times the first, the second digit is twice the first, the third is the sum of the first and second, and the fourth is the sum of the first, second, and third?

ANSWERS

1 FORESIGHT   GIFT HORSE

2   The words are MODE, ROBOT, HARE, HEIGHT, YELLOW, TRAVEL. The letters are M, R, H, H, Y, T, which can be rearranged to spell RHYTHM.

3   They can make thirty-six recycled bottles. They make thirty-one the first time, with four left over. The thirty-one can be turned into four, with three left over, and those seven can be made into one more, for a total of thirty-six.

4   GWENDOLYN is the ony one that cannot be anagrammed. The others can be rearranged as: LETHE, AURAL, HEATERS, CAROLINE.

5   ENID AND EDNA DINE

6   There were 113 peanuts.

7   The missing letter is *W*. The words are UNWISE, SWIVEL, WINNER, WEIGHT, SLOWLY, and GROWTH.

8   MOUNTAINEER

9   341 + 586; 381 + 546; 386 + 541.

10   The missing number is 42. Diamonds are worth twelve, black circles are ten, split circles are nine.

11   A blouse costs $74. The letters are given the value of their position in the alphabet and then summed.

12 PAT AND EDNA TAP

13 TOM, JOHN, BILL, PAT, KEVIN

14 A ROAD MAP TELLS YOU EVERYTHING EXCEPT HOW TO REFOLD IT. (Start at *A* in center.)

15 DROWNING   RING DOWN

16 PUZZLE

17 If the woman were a Liar she would have said she was a Truthteller. If she was really a Truthteller she certainly would have said she was a Truthteller. Therefore, the young man reported truthfully, proving he was a Truthteller. Happy ending.

18 If his top speed is 100 mph he'll never get there. He'll be going 100 mph and be pushed backward at 100 mph. He'll just have to wait until the wind dies down. Of course, if he could get the train up to 150 mph he could do it in four hours, but we've just said 100 mph is the top speed.

19 In ten hours one will have gained a half hour and the other lost a half hour.

20 Daddy, or Pop, or whatever you prefer and he's willing to accept.

21 28463

22 POLAND and DENMARK

23 FACED DEATH   HAD A DEFECT

24 CABBAGES

25 ARILS, RIALS, LIARS, LAIRS, LIRAS, RAILS

26 EGRET, GREBE, CRAKE

27 TURKEY is the odd man out. Each of the others can be anagrammed into the name of a young animal: CALF, POULT, SHOAT, LEVERET

28 The interviewer didn't hire the young man because nobody would say he was a Liar. For a Liar, it would be the truth, which he cannot tell; and for a Truthteller it would be a lie. Therefore, nobody can say that he is a Liar. Also therefore, the young man being interviewed was a Liar.

29 It was 9:00 P.M.

30 WON'T HAVE HIS JOB FOR VERY LONG. (Start at the upper left-hand corner.)

31 Ireland. He only likes words that can be divided into two words.

32 Katie is not an experienced skater. (If she were experienced, she wouldn't be graceless, that is, falling all over the place. Since she is graceless, she cannot be experienced.)

33 CURRANT, PUMPKIN, APPLE

34 A LITTLE LEARNING IS A DANGEROUS THING. (Really A LITTLE KNOWLEDGE . . .) (Start at the *A* in the fourth row down.)

35 SMART

36 *a*). Circles go up one in number each time, triangles go down.

37 C O S T
        O D O R
        S O L O
        T R O T (Of course, there may be other ways.)

38 NIGHTCAP

39 The criminal's memory failed him: 1900 was *not* a leap year. The diary was false.

40 MADE EDAM   TUBE DEBUT

41 DEMURS (RIP, MERMAID, UP, "D," "S," "E")

42 EXTRAVAGANZA   TELEGRAPHER   PROPORTIONAL

43 36421

44 CONTAMINATED   NO ADMITTANCE

45 BEER, BEAR, BEAD, BEND, BENT, DENT, DINT, DINE, WINE. Of course, you may have found a more clever way!

46 COLORADO   SAVANNAH   DELAWARE   ILLINOIS

47 WEDNESDAY

48 Alice is twenty.

49 The number 9. Pairs around the circle (moving clockwise) add up to 13.

50 KLAXON

51 PINE. The second word starts with the second letter, *E*, of the preceding word. The third word starts with the third letter of the second word, the fourth starts with the fourth letter of the third, so the fifth word would start with the fifth letter—*T*. Therefore the sixth word would start with the sixth letter of the preceding word, *P*.

52 SPOLIATION

53 One and one-half hours. The second candle is irrelevant.

54 The right answer is 27. Square the first digit of each entry and add the second number.

55 *b*)

56 Sixteen days. He spends one dollar a day and I spend two dollars.

57 HOT SOUP   SHOOT-UP

58 A. 30. It is a series of the initials of the months and the number of days in each.

59 60 and 24

60 They had to wait twenty minutes.

61 TYPEWRITER

62 FEAR, BEAR, BOAR, BOAT, BOLT, BOLD

63 It was fifteen miles, at three miles per letter.

64 IN THE SPRING A YOUNG MAN'S FANCY LIGHTLY TURNS TO THOUGHTS OF LOVE.

65 TULIP

66 BOOK. (Of course, there may be another answer.)

67 ASCENT   ENACTS   STANCE   SECANT

68 Seventy-five cents

69 NINETY. The last letter of each word starts the next word.

70 Hello, husband.

71 69382

72 The dog weighed one hundred fifty pounds.

73 Nine minutes. You only have to make nine cuts to get ten sections.

74 DWARFS

75 THIS IS HARD BECAUSE THERE ARE THREE CHOICES FOR EACH NUMBER.

76 BUT THE DOORBELL RANG: THAT CLEVER DOG HAD ORDERED A MEAL BY PHONE. (Start at the upper left-hand corner.)

77 There were twelve in the group.

78 COLD, CORD, WORD, WARD, WARM

79 CODDLES   SCOLDED

80 MA HANDED EDNA HAM

81 DELIA WAS ILL, LISA WAILED

82 EARTHLING   LATHERING

83 SIDE

84 A COMMITTEE IS A GROUP WHICH KEEPS MINUTES BUT WASTES HOURS.

85 The proofreader needs thirty-six minutes.

86 QUEUE

87 $345 \times 78 = 26,910$

88 $757 + 757 + 45 = 1,559$

89 None of them can be a Truthteller. The first man's statement cannot be true. If the second says something to indicate the first man is truthful, he is a Liar. The first man cannot be right. The second man is a Liar, as demonstrated, so the third man, who says the second man is telling the truth, must be a Liar. It is possible that the second man is a Truthteller, but he can't really be because the third man says the second is telling the truth, and he is a proven liar. Therefore the second man is also lying. Check each one's statements against the others.

90 There are ten of each coin.

91 AND I AM NONE OF THE ABOVE. (Start with the *A* on the last line.)

92 They've driven 224 miles.

93 TOIL, FOIL, FOOL, FOOD

94 DAISY

95 The correct number is 3. Start at the upper right, add the first three numbers counterclockwise, and divide by the number at lower right.

96 HEARTINESS

97 They started with $250.

98 KOALA OK

99 Four. Try it out for yourself.

100 The missing number is 7. This is not only simple math, but the numbers have been assigned a value corresponding to their alphabetical position; A = 1, B = 2, and so on.

101 24198

102 The missing letter is *M*. Starting at the upper right, the squares read, SOME TASKS ARE EASIER THAN THEY SEEM.

103 MARGE LETS NORAH SEE SHARON'S TELEGRAM

104 TEAL   SHRIKE   GROUSE

105 *B* and *G*

106 WRONG

107 THINK

108 KIPLING, KEATS, SWINBURNE

109 Because if you have 1991 dollars you have one more dollar than if you have 1990.

110 MEAT, BEAT, BOAT, BOLT, BOLE, BONE

111 JUST ASK A FAILURE, HE WILL TELL YOU SO. (Start at the only *J*—second line.)

112 The names are MILLICENT, LAURA, and ANGELINA. QUARK—which is not normally a girl's name—is the odd one out.

113 The correct answer was 95.

114 LEW, OTTO HAS A HOT TOWEL

115 She started with $64.

116 Ten and eight

117 TESSA'S IN ITALY, LATIN IS ASSET

118 CROUTONS TUBER PEARS CHICKEN ENDIVE

119 The second man is the Liar, because if he is telling the truth then there are two Truthtellers, which cannot be. If the first man's statement is correct, the second man cannot both agree and contradict; and if it is false and the second man is a Truthteller, then he would have to say that the first man's statement was false, but he didn't. So the first man is a Truthteller and the second is a Liar.

120 13245. This is just a simple substitution code.

121 They'll get seventy-five cans: seventy-two the first time around and another three from those recycled.

122 TONGA MALTA NEPAL

123 Yourself

124 1 3 81

125 25. Black circles are worth five points, split circles six, split triangles seven, and black triangles eight.

126 Tulips. She only likes words in which two consecutive letters of the alphabet appear.

127 PARABLES

128 WORD, WOLD, WELD, WEED, DEED

129 PEERESSES ABRACADABRA EPHEMERA PRESENTABLE INVIGILATED

130 SOFTSIDED SOFTWARE SOFT TOUCH SOFTWOOD SOFT-SHOE (and many others) BEDPOST POSTMAN BOOK POST POSTHOLE (also many others) DOORFRAME DOORPOST DOORWAY DOORJAMB READJUST READMIT READHERE READABLE

131 c). It's the area below the overlaid figure.

132 The sisters are fifty-two and thirty-nine.

133 LONG, LONE, LINE, WINE, WIDE

134 CLEANLINESS IS NEXT TO IMPOSSIBLE. (Alphabet numbered backward is the code.)

135 927 × 63 = 58,401

136 "IF IT COMES OUT RIGHT, YOU'VE DONE IT WRONG." (Start at the top left corner.)

137 Samantha and Sally had $100.

138 He is abstemious. He only likes words with all five vowels in them.

139 MIND. Place the letters of the alphabet in the grid, from left to right in normal order. Z is outside the grid. Then read off and unscramble the letters that have been blacked out.

140 RIGHT. You can go back and see which errors you made in crossing out those letters.

141 DIAL

142 BED   KEY   HORSE

143 A PENNY SAVED IS A PENNY EARNED.

144 There were ten people; each received five dollars. The total was fifty dollars.

145 SIMPLE DIET   SPEED LIMIT

146 The items cost four dollars, six dollars, twelve dollars, and six dollars.

147 40 mph and 120 miles distance

148 The missing number is 10. Add the pair of digits and multiply by 2.

149 They ordered two hundred fifty dresses.

150 CROSS   FALL   KIND

151
4½	8	2½
3	5	7
7½	2	5½

152 The couples spent $40, $70, and $10, for a total of $120.

153 Tortoise 1, who races at six miles per day, will always win, regardless of the distance involved. He takes exactly two days; Tortoise 2 takes two and one-quarter days. It is mathematically impossible to make up the time lost going uphill.

154 PROSELYTE

155 17

156 Well, if she sold one for twenty dollars and made a 25 percent profit, that was 125 percent of the cost, so it cost her sixteen dollars and she made four dollars. On the other hand, if she paid twenty dollars and sold it for 25 percent off, she'd be selling it for fifteen dollars. So she lost one dollar on the deal.

157

```
  1 2 3 4 5 6 7 9
            × 9
  ───────────────
  1 1 1 1 1 1 1 1 1
```

158 ASH LARCH CEDAR

159 PLAY, PLAT, BLAT, BOAT, BOLT, BOLD, WOLD, WORD, WORK. Of course, there are other ways.

160 APPLE PEACH BANANA
PORK VEAL BEEF
SQUASH RUTABAGA BEET

161 BIRDS OF A FEATHER FLOCK TOGETHER.
A FOOL AND HIS MONEY ARE SOON PARTED.

162 MISTRESS MARY QUITE CONTRARY. Start at the upper left of the first box and go counterclockwise and then to the middle. The missing letter is Y.

163 The words are GALE, LADDERS, HERO, CASA, ILK, and TOMORROW. The new word is GLITCH.

164 715 × 46 = 32,890

165 You can't put a piece of paper between an odd and even page. Odd pages are always on the right. Therefore, the suspect was lying.

166 All can be anagrammed except PUPPY. The words are HARKS, GREET, AMBER, and PRIDES.

167 She lived sixty miles away.

168 A widget costs two dollars, a wonkle costs three.

169 Six puzzle solvers are needed.

170 BLOWING A WHISTLE   WITH A SINGLE BLOW

171 *c)*. The pattern is the alphabet forward, then backward.

172 FOOLS RUSH IN WHERE ANGELS FEAR TO TREAD.

173 TENET. It's the only one that can't be rearranged into another word. The others are ABODE SLAVE TODAY DIVAN LOYAL

174 CONFRONTING   INACCURACY   PREVENTABLE

175 12365

DR. ABBIE SALNY has had a long and successful career as one of America's top puzzle makers. She has authored or coauthored six best-selling Mensa puzzle books between 1981 and 1991. In addition, she is the acclaimed author of *Brain Busters* and *Cranium Crackers,* and the original *Supersmart Superpuzzle Book* for Dell. Abbie Salny is a retired professor and deputy chairman of the psychology department at Montclair State College. She is also supervisory psychologist for American and International Mensa, in charge of all testing. She lives in New Jersey.